Withdrawn

ZOE SALDANA

Maggie Murphy

PowerKiDS
press
New York

Published in 2011 by The Rosen Publishing Group, Inc.
29 East 21st Street, New York, NY 10010

First Edition

Editor: Jennifer Way
Book Design: Kate Laczynski

Photo Credits: Cover Kristian Dowling/Getty Images; pp. 4, 6, 24, 25 Jason Merritt/Getty Images; p. 5 Astrid Stawiarz/Getty Images; pp. 7 (top), 10 Shutterstock.com; p. 7 (bottom) Mychal Watts/WireImage/Getty Images; pp. 9, 12 © Columbia Pictures Corporation/Zuma Press; p. 11 R.J. Capak/WireImage/Getty Images; pp. 14, 26 Kevin Winter/Getty Images; p. 15 Anthony Harvey/Getty Images; pp. 16, 29 Vince Bucci/Getty Images; p. 17 Pascal Le Segretain/Getty Images; pp. 18–19, 22 Andreas Rentz/Getty Images; p. 20 Claire Greenway/Getty Images; p. 21 Toshifumi Kitamura/AFP/Getty Images; p. 23 © 20th Century Fox/Everett Digital; p. 27 Stephen Lovekin/Getty Images; p. 28 Gabriel Bouys/AFP/Getty Images; p. 30 Alberto E. Rodriguez/Getty Images.

Library of Congress Cataloging-in-Publication Data

Murphy, Maggie.
  Zoe Saldana / by Maggie Murphy. — 1st ed.
      p. cm. — (Movie superstars)
  Includes index.
  ISBN 978-1-4488-2565-3 (library binding) — ISBN 978-1-4488-2719-0 (pbk.) —
  ISBN 978-1-4488-2720-6 (6-pack)
  1. Saldana, Zoë—Juvenile literature. 2. Actors—United States—Biography—Juvenile
  literature. I. Title.
  PN2287.S255M76 2011
  791.4302'8092—dc22
  [B]
                                            2010031984

Manufactured in the United States of America

CPSIA Compliance Information: Batch #WW11PK: For Further Information contact Rosen Publishing, New York, New York at 1-800-237-9932

☆ Contents

Zoe Saldana started out as a dancer and then acted in theater before making movies.

Zoe Saldana is an award-winning movie actress. She is best known for playing strong female characters, such as Uhura in *Star Trek* and Neytiri in *Avatar*. She has also appeared in several other movies, including *Crossroads* and *Pirates of the Caribbean: The Curse of the Black Pearl*.

Saldana was born in New Jersey and grew up in New York City and the Dominican Republic. She studied dance for many years before she began acting. This helped her get roles in movies such as *Center Stage* and *Drumline*. Saldana also enjoys working for good causes and spending time with her friends and family.

Zoe Saldana likes to spend her free time with her family and friends. Here she is with her fiancé Keith Britton.

Here is Saldana with her mother, Asalia Nazario.

Zoe Saldana was born on June 19, 1978, in Passaic, New Jersey. Her name when she was born was Zoe Yadira Zaldana Nazario. Saldana is of Caribbean **ancestry**. Her mother is Puerto Rican and her father is Dominican. Saldana spent most of her childhood living in New York City.

However, when Zoe was 10, her family moved to the Dominican Republic. There, she studied ballet, jazz, and modern dance at one of the country's best dance schools.

Saldana has two sisters, named Mariel and Cisely. Growing up, Saldana enjoyed playing volleyball with her sisters. She also practiced archery in her spare time.

Above: *The Dominican Republic, shown here, is a country in the Caribbean.* Left: *Here is Zoe (center) with her two sisters, Cisely (left) and Mariel (right).*

STAGE CAREER

Zoe Saldana moved back to New York City with her family when she was 17. There, she became interested in performing in the theater as well as dancing. Zoe joined a theater troupe, or group, called FACES. FACES put on positive **improvisational** skits about choices and problems that teenagers living in New York might face, such as drug use. Saldana enjoyed performing in this troupe. She also enjoyed being a role model for other teenagers and having a positive **impact** on their lives.

Saldana's experience as a dancer helped her win a role in the 2000 movie Center Stage.

SUPERSTAR FACT

Zoe Saldana speaks both English and Spanish.

Saldana also joined another theater troupe called the New York Youth Theater. This theater troupe put on performances of plays, such as *Joseph and the Amazing Technicolor*

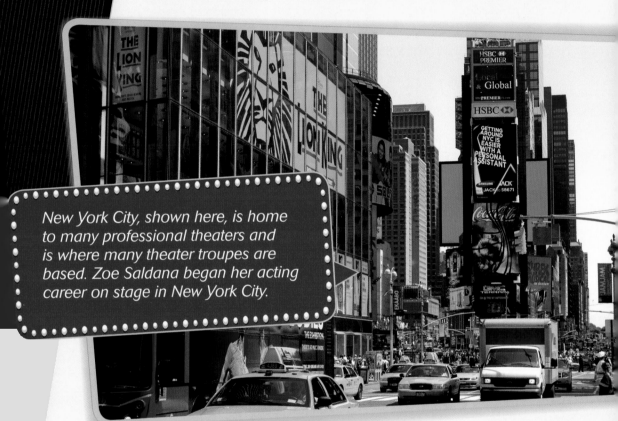

New York City, shown here, is home to many professional theaters and is where many theater troupes are based. Zoe Saldana began her acting career on stage in New York City.

Dreamcoat. While Saldana was a part of the New York Youth Theater, her acting got the notice of a talent **agent**. The talent agent thought Saldana could find success acting on television and in movies.

0

GETTING INTO MOVIES

One of Zoe Saldana's first acting experiences on TV was on a show called *Law & Order*. She played a small role on an episode of the show in 1999.

However, in 2000, Saldana appeared in a much larger role in *Center Stage*, a movie about young ballet dancers who want to make it into

One of Saldana's first movie roles was in Center Stage. *Here she is at the opening of that movie.*

a famous ballet company. Saldana played a character named Eva Rodriguez, a dancer who has trouble listening to her teachers. This was one of Saldana's **breakout** roles. It got the notice of moviegoers, **critics**, directors, and **producers**. Like many of the actors in the movie, Saldana was cast in *Center Stage* partly because of her ballet training.

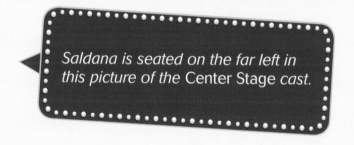

Saldana is seated on the far left in this picture of the Center Stage *cast.*

After her first big movie role, in *Center Stage*, Saldana had smaller parts in two more films in 2001. She appeared in *Get Over It*, a romantic comedy starring Kirsten Dunst, as well as *Snipes*, a movie starring the rapper Nelly.

Crossroads *is a movie about a group of friends. Taryn Manning (right) played Mimi, and Saldana (left) played Kit.*

Zoe Saldana had even more success as a movie actress in 2002 and 2003. In 2002, Saldana costarred with Britney Spears in a movie called *Crossroads*. *Crossroads* was about three friends, Lucy, Kit, and Mimi, who go on a road trip to Los

Angeles after they have graduated from high school. Saldana plays Kit, the high school's prom queen who is engaged to be married.

Saldana also had a role in a 2002 movie called *Drumline*, starring Nick Cannon. *Drumline* was about a competition between college marching bands. Saldana played Laila, a captain of one of the marching bands' dance teams. Nick Cannon's character, Devon, falls in love with Laila. Saldana's

Britney Spears plays Luc... in Crossroads. *Here she is at that movie's openin... with Anson Mount, who also costars in the mov...*

Saldana appeared in Pirates of the Caribbean: The Curse of the Black Pearl *with Orlando Bloom. The two actors were both in the movie* Haven.

dance training helped her in this role. In 2003, Saldana also had a **supporting** role in *Pirates of the Caribbean: The Curse of the Black Pearl*, starring Johnny Depp, Orlando Bloom, and Keira Knightley. She played a female pirate named Anamaria.

STAR TREK

After getting noticed by fans, critics, and moviemakers in her first few movie roles, Zoe Saldana continued to act between 2004 and 2008. She appeared in several movies, including *The Terminal*, and had guest roles on television shows such as *Six Degrees* during this time.

Another big break for Saldana came in the summer of 2009, when she appeared in the movie *Star Trek. Star Trek* was based on a popular television

Steven Spielberg (left) directed The Terminal, which starred Tom Hanks (right). Saldana played a supporting ro[le] in the movie.

Here is the cast of Star Trek. From left to right are John Cho, Eric Bana, Karl Urban, Saldana, director J. J. Abrams, Zachary Quinto, Simon Pegg, and Chris Pine.

show of the same name about the crew of a spaceship called the *Enterprise*. The movie starred Chris Pine and Zachary Quinto. In *Star Trek*, Saldana played Uhura, an important member of the *Enterprise's* crew who **specializes** in different languages.

Many people in the media called the 2009 *Star Trek* movie a **reboot** of the original *Star Trek* series. The movie had a lot of

SUPERSTAR FACT

Zoe Saldana says that she has always been a fan of science-fiction movies.

action **sequences** and exciting special effects
that drew movie **audiences** who had never
seen the original series. The movie was a huge
box-office success, making more than $385

Here is Zoe at the London premiere of Star Trek.

million worldwide. Saldana did many interviews in magazines and on television about her role in *Star Trek*. Fans and critics took notice of Saldana's acting in the movie and were excited for her next role, in *Avatar*.

AVATAR

After her breakout role in *Star Trek*, Zoe Saldana starred in an Academy Award-winning **science-fiction** movie called *Avatar* in December 2009. *Avatar* was directed by James Cameron and costarred Sam Worthington. The movie takes place on a moon called Pandora. The Na'vi, the people who live on the moon, are very tall, bright blue, and have catlike ears. Saldana plays a Na'vi warrior named Neytiri.

Saldana (left) and Sam Worthington (right) starred in 2009's Avatar. The movie made $2.7 billion and made Saldana a household name.

James Cameron (right) directed Avatar. *Sigourney Weaver (left) played a supporting role in the movie.*

Avatar was made with motion-capture technology, which required many of the actors, including Saldana, to perform wearing special motion-capture suits and helmets. The suits and helmets allowed their body movements to be captured by special cameras and turned into

To create the character of Neytiri, Saldana wore a motion-capture suit and helmet. Computers then turned the information from the suit into what people saw on the screen.

Na'vi bodies through **computer generation**. In order to play Neytiri, Saldana had to go through training in martial arts, archery, and horseback riding. She has said that her dance training and love of archery helped prepare her for the role.

Avatar made $2.7 billion worldwide and won three 2010 Academy Awards. Saldana was **nominated** for several awards for her role in *Avatar*. Many film critics and fans now consider Saldana an A-list Hollywood actress.

SALDANA'S AWARDS

Zoe Saldana has been nominated for several awards during her acting career. She was nominated for an MTV Movie Award in 2003 and a Teen Choice Award in 2005. In 2009, Saldana was nominated for another Teen Choice Award for her role in *Star Trek*. In 2010, Saldana was nominated for a People's Choice Award and two MTV Movie Awards.

Now that she is an A-list actress, Saldana attends many awards ceremonies. Here she is at the 2010 Kids' Choice Awards.

Saldana has also won awards for her acting performances. Saldana won an Empire Award, a British acting award, for her role in *Avatar* in 2010. She was also named Film Actress of the Year at the 2010 Glamour Women of the Year Awards.

Here is Saldana (right) with Zac Efron (left) at the 2010 Critic's Choice Awards.

FASHION AND CHARITY WORK

Saldana is very interested in fashion. Here she is at the 2010 Costume Institute Gala, at the Metropolitan Museum of Art, in New York City.

Zoe Saldana has many other interests besides acting, including fashion. Saldana has posed in fashion spreads in magazines. She has also attended fashion events, such as the Costume Institute Gala, at the Metropolitan Museum of Art, in New York City.

Saldana has worked to help the homeless. Here she is helping serve Thanksgiving dinner in Los Angeles in 2009.

Saldana also does **philanthropic** work. She worked to raise money for Haitian earthquake victims in 2010. In April 2010, she was honored by St. Jude Children's Research Hospital, in Memphis, for her work raising money for that hospital. Saldana wants to work more with groups that support children with **autism** and Iraq War veterans.

SALDANA'S FUTURE

Zoe Saldana has many fans from her roles in *Star Trek* and *Avatar*. She starred in two action movies in 2010, *The Losers* and *Takers*. Both movies featured fight scenes and lots of action.

In the future, Saldana hopes to become an action heroine. The future holds many more exciting movie roles for Saldana, such as a possible *Avatar* sequel. In 2011, Saldana starred in an action movie called

When she is walking the red carpet before events, Saldana takes time to greet her fans.

Here is Saldana at the Los Angeles opening of The Losers.

Columbiana. She will keep playing Uhura in the *Star Trek* movies, in which she will get to do more action scenes. Saldana's fans look forward to seeing her become one of the biggest stars in Hollywood!

Glossary

agent (AY-jent) A person who helps a writer, actor, or sports player with his or her job.

ancestry (AN-ses-tree) The group of people who make up a person's relatives.

audiences (AH-dee-ints-ez) Groups of people who watch or listen to something.

autism (AW-tih-zum) A set of problems some people have that may include trouble dealing with others or talking.

breakout (BRAYK-owt) Having to do with sudden success.

computer generation (kum-PYOO-ter jeh-neh-RAY-shun) Making something using computers.

critics (KRIH-tiks) People who write their opinions about things.

impact (IM-pakt) An effect.

improvisational (im-pro-vuh-ZAY-shnul) Performed without preparation.

nominated (NO-muh-nayt-ed) Suggested that someone or something should be given an award or a position.

philanthropic (fih-lun-THRO-pik) Having to do with goodwill toward others.

producers (pruh-DOO-serz) People who make movies and TV shows.

reboot (ree-BOOT) To restart.

science-fiction (sy-unts-FIK-shun) Work that deals with the effect of real or imagined science.

sequences (SEE-kwens-ez) Things done in a certain order.

specializes (SPEH-shuh-lyz-ez) Does something very well.

supporting (suh-PORT-ing) Acting with someone else.

Index

Web Sites

Due to the changing nature of Internet links, PowerKids Press has developed an online list of Web sites related to the subject of this book. This site is updated regularly. Please use this link to access the list: www.powerkidslinks.com/mss/saldana/